CORIANDER

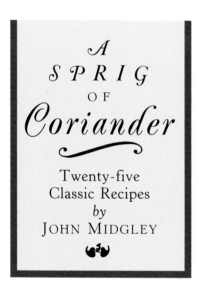

A
S P R I G
O F
Coriander

Twenty-five
Classic Recipes
by
JOHN MIDGLEY

Illustrated *by*
IAN SIDAWAY

A Bulfinch Press Book
Little, Brown and Company
BOSTON · NEW YORK · TORONTO · LONDON

ACKNOWLEDGEMENTS
The author thanks Sue Midgley and Helen Parker for checking the text,
and Ian Sidaway for his excellent illustrations.

FURTHER READING
The Complete Book of Herbs, by Lesley Bremness (Dorling Kindersley)
The Encyclopedia of Herbs, Spices and Flavourings, by Elisabeth Lambert Ortiz
(Dorling Kindersley)
The Herb Book, by Arabella Boxer and Philippa Black (Octopus)
The Herb Garden, by Sarah Garland (Windward)
History of the English Herb Garden, by Kay Sanecki (Ward Lock)
How to Grow and Use Herbs, by Ann Bonar and Daphne MacCarthy
(Ward Lock)
Wisley Handbooks: Culinary Herbs, by Mary Page and William Stearn
(Cassell for the RHS)

First Edition
ISBN 0-8212-2098-5
A CIP catalogue record for this book is available
from the British Library

Conceived and designed by Andrew Barron and John Midgley

Published simultaneously in the United States of America
by Bulfinch Press, an imprint and trademark of
Little, Brown and Company (Inc.),
in Great Britain by Little, Brown and Company (UK) Ltd.
and in Canada by Little, Brown & Company (Canada) Limited

PRINTED AND BOUND IN ITALY

CONTENTS

CORIANDER

CORIANDER

Coriander (*Coriandrum sativum*) is related to the carrot and belongs to the *Umbelliferae* family of plants. Many other herbs belong to this large group, including angelica, anise, caraway, chervil, cumin, dill, fennel, lovage, parsley, and sweet cicely.

'Coriander' derives from *koris*, the ancient Greek word for insect. In the USA, it is usually called by its Spanish name, *cilantro*, while in Britain it is also known as 'Chinese parsley'. Native to the eastern Mediterranean, coriander was grown by the ancient Egyptians (and very probably by earlier peoples). It has been cultivated continuously ever since. Among several biblical references attesting to the

plant's long-standing religious importance is a description of manna from heaven which is likened to white coriander seeds.

The Romans appreciated coriander and introduced it into northern and western Europe where, for centuries, the seeds have been used to flavour marinades and sauces. They have also long been valued medicinally, particularly as an aid to digestion. The Spaniards took coriander on board their voyages of discovery and introduced the plant into the New World where it is still very popular today, especially in Mexico.

Coriander seeds and the fresh leaves are both ancient and ubiquitous flavouring ingredients in the Balkans, North Africa, Arabia, India, China and throughout south-east Asia. In the latter region, the roots are ground together with spices and other indigenous flavourings such as kaffir lime leaves and lemon grass to make curry pastes.

A hardy annual, coriander will grow to a height of 60 cm/2 feet. The top leaves are thin and feathery, very similar to carrot fronds, but the more desirable lower ones are larger, with a characteristic indented trifoliate shape that is easily confused with flat-leaved parsley. The small, pink-ish-white flowers bloom profusely, leaving large, round seeds that smell unpleasant until they have matured; then, their pleasant, spicy aroma is reminiscent of orange peel. All other parts of the plant are strong-smelling; the distinctive fragrance of coriander has been described variously as 'warm', 'pungent', 'musky', and 'orangey'.

GROWING CORIANDER

Coriander is best sown from seed, although potted plants are now widely available. Even seeds taken from the spice jar will germinate fairly readily. A sunny position is essential; the plants need plenty of warmth, and shelter from cold winds. The seeds should be sown in April into well-drained, fertile soil at $\frac{1}{2}$ cm/$\frac{1}{4}$ inch intervals. Seedlings should be thinned out to leave a gap of about 12 cm/5 inches between plants. If coriander is grown for its seeds, it will be ready for harvesting in late summer, but it is imperative to wait until the seeds smell pleasantly spicy. If grown as a leaf herb, however, once the plants have adequate foliage, the broad lower leaves can be picked whenever they are required and picking will encourage new growth. Drying the leaves is not worthwhile.

Coriander plants are normally free of pests and diseases. Being vigorous, and needing little care other than regular watering to encourage profuse growth of the lower leaves, coriander is an ideal herb to grow, whether in containers or in herb beds.

CORIANDER

COOKING WITH CORIANDER

Until relatively recently many cookery books published in the West have referred to coriander only as a spice, and not as a herb. However, the fast-growing popularity of exotic cuisines has put fresh coriander firmly on the culinary map. The herb has found favour with creative domestic cooks and illustrious professional chefs alike. In fact, it would be fair to describe fresh coriander as a 'fashionable' ingredient, although its ability to transform a dish completely, and to impart a deliciously warm flavour and fragrance, will guarantee it a permanent place in our kitchens.

There are three essential culinary uses of coriander. The first is to add the fresh leaves to dishes as a garnish or flavouring just before serving. The wonderful deep, warm flavour complements a whole range of ingredients, from lamb and beef to seafood and vegetables. The leaves are also good in salads. Leaf coriander is especially appropriate in all manner of Chinese stir-fries and braises, oriental noodles, Indian and south-east Asian curries and soups, hot Mexican *salsas*, and various Middle Eastern dishes. The second is to use the well-washed roots, particularly when making curry pastes. (When buying coriander, always check that the roots are still attached – they are not only a wonderful ingredient, they will also help to keep the leaves fresh a little longer.) The third is to use the seeds, which have an altogether different, spicier aroma and flavour. They may be added whole to marinades, sauces, chutneys, pickles and relishes; or they can be ground and added to

Indian and south-east Asian curries (sometimes they are lightly toasted first).

In Indian cookery ground coriander and cumin seeds are inseparable companions, and often the seeds and the leaves are used in the same dish, each lending distinct characteristics at different stages of preparation. Coriander seeds are also an essential ingredient in commercial brands of curry powder and paste, and they are also used in Western baking and confectionery.

As it is so powerful, coriander may overwhelm delicate ingredients such as poultry and fish, especially when they are relatively blandly cooked in the Western manner. It is unwise, therefore, to be over-generous when garnishing such dishes. On the other hand, Chinese cooks add liberal quantities to hearty stews and stir-fries, particularly when they wish to mask the over-assertive flavours of certain meats such as lamb. The strong flavour and heady perfume of the fresh leaves is wonderful in highly-flavoured soups such as the delicious Thai seafood broth called *tom yam gung* (see page 20). In general, coriander is best in spicy, pungent and highly-flavoured food.

A bunch of coriander will keep well for a few days if the roots or stems are plunged into a jug or vase of cold water. (Ensure, however, that the lower leaves are not submerged.) Alternatively, store the leaves in the refrigerator, wrapped in a food bag. Avoid buying coriander if you detect any of the following defects: limp, yellowing leaves; dark, bruised leaves which will rapidly turn slimy; a greater proportion of feathery top leaves to broad lower ones; or tops that have obviously bolted and developed tiny flowering buds.

Store coriander seeds in an air-tight container to preserve their perfume. If harvesting your own seeds, hang the whole tops of the mature plants in a warm, airy place; when the foliage has dried completely, shake out the seeds and store them.

Most of the following recipes are traditional dishes culled from countries as diverse as China, Thailand, India and Mexico with a few of my own creations added to the pot for good measure.

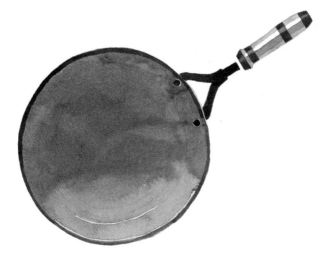

CORIANDER RELISH

This delicious hot relish complements almost any Indian dish. It also goes well with *crudités*. Makes enough for 6 people.

4–6 hot green chili peppers, washed and seeded
2 handfuls of coriander leaves
1 clove of garlic, peeled and chopped
½ tsp cumin seeds
½ tsp coriander seeds
½ tsp salt
2 tbs water
1 tbs lime or lemon juice
110 ml/4 fl oz/½ cup strained live yoghurt
white parts of 2 spring onions (scallions), washed and very thinly sliced

In a food processor, liquidize all the ingredients except for the yoghurt and the spring onions. Beat the yoghurt with a fork until it is thick and creamy. Fold in the spring onions and the liquidized coriander mixture. Set aside for 30 minutes or longer before serving.

CORIANDER CHUTNEY

Desiccated (dried and shredded) coconut gives this chutney a very distinctive flavour and texture. Traditionally, coriander chutney is served with *samosas* and *bhajias*, although it can accompany most Indian dishes.

110 ml/4 fl oz/½ cup strained yoghurt
25 g/1 oz desiccated coconut
1 tsp salt
1 tsp sugar
1 tbs lime or lemon juice
1 clove of garlic, peeled
4 hot green chili peppers, seeded and washed
generous handful of coriander leaves, washed

Beat the yoghurt with a fork. Mix in the desiccated coconut, salt, sugar, and lime or lemon juice. Chop the remaining ingredients very finely, then fold them into the yoghurt. Serve immediately or within 1 hour.

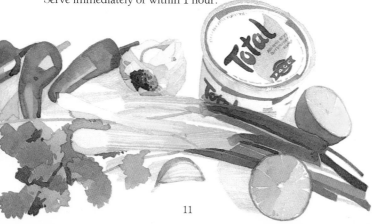

11

$\mathscr{L}$ÉGUMES À LA GRECQUE

The suffix *à la grecque* refers to the French technique of marinating vegetables and mushrooms cooked in olive oil with pickling spices. Usually only a single vegetable is prepared in this way but the following combination offers interesting flavours and textures. Serves 6 people.

450 g/1 lb courgettes (zucchini), washed
salt
12 pickling onions or shallots, peeled
225 g/8 oz button mushrooms, wiped clean
225 g/8 oz celery, trimmed and cut into 2 cm/1 inch chunks
110 ml/4 fl oz/½ cup olive oil
110 ml/4 fl oz/½ cup white wine
1 tbs red wine or sherry vinegar
2 tbs tomato purée (paste)
1 tsp black peppercorns, lightly crushed
1 tsp coriander seeds
2 bay leaves
sprig of thyme
1 tsp salt
4 sprigs of coriander

Cut the courgettes into even chunks. Sprinkle with salt and let them 'bleed' for 20 minutes while you prepare the remaining ingredients. Rinse and pat them dry. Put all the ingredients into a saucepan except for the sprigs of coriander. Bring to the boil, cover the pan, reduce the heat and simmer for 25 minutes. Transfer to a serving bowl, cover and refrigerate. Serve several hours later (or the following day), garnished with the sprigs of coriander.

12

MARINATED MUSHROOMS WITH CORIANDER

These mushrooms make an excellent *hors d'oeuvre* or appetizer for 4 people, accompanied by toasted slices of French bread. Use different mushrooms such as oyster, shiitake, chestnut and white buttons, slicing large ones coarsely but leaving small ones whole.

3 tbs olive oil
4 shallots or *a small onion, peeled and very finely chopped*
2 cloves of garlic, peeled and chopped
2 tbs canned tomatoes, chopped or *3 tbs crushed tomatoes*
110 ml/4 fl oz/½ cup white wine
2 tbs lemon juice
salt and freshly milled black pepper
sprigs of thyme and marjoram
2 tsp hot paprika or *1 tsp sweet paprika and ½ tsp cayenne*
350 g/12 oz firm, very fresh mushrooms, cleaned and trimmed
leaves from 6 sprigs of coriander, washed and chopped

Heat the oil in a pan. Sauté the shallots until soft and translucent, then add the garlic and the remaining ingredients except for the mushrooms and the coriander. Cover the pan and simmer for 25 minutes. Add the mushrooms and cook with the lid on for an additional 5 minutes. Stir in the coriander and allow to cool. Transfer the contents to a large bowl, cover and leave to marinate for 12–24 hours. Serve cold.

$\mathscr{S}$ALAD WITH FRESH HERBS

This Turkish salad can be assembled with whatever delicious seasonal salad vegetables are available. Served on its own, it makes an excellent appetizer, and it can also be enjoyed as an accompaniment to barbecued or grilled (broiled) meat or poultry. Add quartered hard-boiled eggs, black olives and some anchovy fillets to give the salad a rustic western Mediterranean character. Serves 4 people.

1 cos (romaine) lettuce
1 green pepper
6–8 spring onions (scallions)
10–12 radishes
4 tomatoes
1 small Mediterranean cucumber or $\frac{1}{2}$ a cucumber
handful of rocket (arugula) leaves
6 sprigs of coriander
6 sprigs of mint
6 sprigs of parsley
4–6 tbs extra virgin olive oil
juice of $\frac{1}{2}$ a lemon
1 tsp salt

Wash all the vegetables and herbs, shaking off as much moisture as possible. Pat them dry with kitchen paper (paper towel). Discard the limp outer leaves of the lettuce, break up the crisp leaves and the heart and place them in a salad bowl. Remove the cap, pith and seeds of the pepper, slice into thin rings and put them to one side. Trim off the

bottoms and the green parts of the spring onions, slice the white parts thickly and set aside. Trim and quarter the radishes. Remove the tomatoes' caps and slice thickly. Trim and peel the cucumber, leaving long, thin strips of peel to give an attractive striped effect. Slice thinly and combine with all the prepared vegetables and the rocket leaves. Remove the stalks from the herbs and add the leaves to the salad. Beat the olive oil, lemon juice and salt until creamy. Pour over the salad, mix thoroughly, and serve straight away.

15

Hummus

Traditionally this very popular salad of chick peas (garbanzos) puréed with olive oil, lemon juice, garlic and spices is served with *pitta* bread. Sometimes *tahini* (sesame paste) is added but I prefer the simpler version which I garnish with fresh coriander and a pinch of cayenne.

1 tbs olive oil
2 large cloves of garlic, peeled and halved
400 g/14 oz can of chick peas, rinsed and drained
6 tbs fresh lemon juice
2 tbs water
110 ml/4 fl oz/½ cup extra virgin olive oil
2 tsp ground cumin
½ tsp cayenne
small handful of fresh coriander, washed and chopped

Heat 1 tbs of olive oil in a small pan. Add the garlic and fry gently and briefly. Remove the garlic before it browns and combine it in a food processor with the chick peas, lemon juice, water, most of the extra virgin olive oil and the cumin. Blend to a smooth paste. Divide between 4 bowls, dress with additional olive oil to taste, sprinkle with cayenne and garnish with coriander. Serve with *crudités* and warm *pitta* bread.

THAI CARROT AND CUCUMBER SALAD

This hot, sweet and sour salad normally accompanies *satay* but it is equally good with more elaborate oriental dishes. Alternatively, serve it as an appetizer. Makes enough for 4 people.

½ cucumber, peeled and halved from end to end
2 medium carrots, peeled and halved from end to end
2 tbs sugar
2 tbs rice vinegar
1 tbs light soy sauce
2 shallots, peeled and thinly sliced
1-2 fresh chili peppers, seeded and thinly sliced
handful of fresh coriander, washed and chopped
50 g/2 oz roasted peanuts, lightly crushed

Slice the cucumber and carrots very thinly and put them into a bowl. Stirring thoroughly, dissolve the sugar in the vinegar and soy sauce. Pour in the liquid, scatter the shallots, chilies, coriander and peanuts over the vegetables and serve straight away.

CARROT AND CORIANDER SOUP

This delicious soup marries together very successfully the contrasting flavours of coriander seeds and the plant's fresh leaves. Surprisingly thick and creamy, it is packed full of goodness and can be frozen. Serves 4 people.

50 g/2 oz butter
350 g/12 oz carrots, peeled and chopped
1 large onion, peeled and chopped
3 sticks (ribs) of celery, washed and chopped
salt and freshly milled black pepper
2 tsp ground coriander
1 tsp ground cumin
900 ml/2 pints/4 cups chicken stock (broth)
handful of fresh coriander, washed and finely chopped

Melt the butter in a large pot. Stir-fry the vegetables for about 10 minutes over a medium heat to soften them. Add the seasoning and spices and fry for 1 minute longer. Add the stock and bring to the boil. Reduce the heat, cover and simmer for 30 minutes. Allow the soup to cool, then liquidize it. Re-heat it gently without boiling. Garnish with the coriander leaves and serve with bread or croûtons.

$\mathscr{S}$OPA DE FRIJOL

This substantial, very thick Mexican bean soup is deservedly popular. It is extremely nourishing, thoroughly satisfying – almost a meal in itself – and may also be frozen. Serves 4 people.

3 tbs vegetable oil
1 onion, peeled and chopped
2 cloves of garlic, peeled and chopped
2 fresh chili peppers, seeded and chopped
800 g/1³/₄ lb canned or cooked red kidney beans, drained
400 g/14 oz canned tomatoes, chopped
900 ml/2 pints/4 cups chicken stock (broth)
juice of 1 lime
salt and freshly milled black pepper
handful of fresh coriander, washed and chopped

Heat the oil in a large, lidded pan. Fry the onion, garlic and chili peppers until soft. Add the beans and tomatoes, mix well and simmer for 3 minutes. Pour in the stock and lime juice, season and bring to the boil. Cover the pan, reduce the heat and simmer for 30 minutes. Remove the lid, allow the soup to cool and liquidize in a food processor. Re-heat it gently and stir in the coriander just before serving. Serve with broken *tortilla* chips or croûtons.

$\mathcal{T}$OM YAM GUNG

This most popular of Thai soups is deliciously hot, sour and fragrant. This excellent recipe serves 4 people and may be offered to guests along with other Thai dishes or as a starter.

450 g/1 lb raw, unshelled prawns (shrimps)
900 ml/2 pints/4 cups chicken stock
tender part of 1 stalk of lemon grass, sliced
2 kaffir lime leaves or a twist of lime or lemon peel
2 tbs lime or lemon juice
1 tbs light soy sauce
1 tbs Chinese chili sauce
225 g/8 oz button mushrooms, very thinly sliced
2 fresh red chili peppers, seeded and thinly sliced
2 spring onions (scallions), trimmed and thinly sliced
handful of fresh coriander, washed and chopped

Wash and peel the prawns. Put the shells into a pot with the stock, lemon grass, citrus leaves (or peel) and the juice. Bring to the boil, reduce the heat, cover and simmer for 15 minutes. Strain the soup. Re-heat it and add the peeled prawns, the soy and chili sauces, mushrooms, chilies and spring onions. Heat without boiling, cover the pot and simmer gently for 2–3 minutes. Add the coriander and serve at once.

GREEN BEANS WITH CORIANDER

Serve these delicious, spicy beans with any simple fish, poultry or meat dish. If using matchstick green beans reduce the cooking time accordingly; the beans, although tender should remain very slightly crunchy. They serve 4 people as a vegetable accompaniment.

450 g/1 lb green beans, washed
2 tbs vegetable oil
2 cloves of garlic, peeled and chopped
1 dried red chili pepper, crumbled
1 tsp coriander seeds, ground
1 tsp cumin seeds, ground
splash of white wine
225 g/8 oz ripe tomatoes (or canned plum tomatoes), peeled and chopped
salt and freshly milled black pepper
handful of fresh coriander, washed and chopped

Top and tail the beans. Heat the oil in a lidded pan; add the beans, garlic, chili and ground spices. Stir them around for 2 minutes, taking care not to burn the garlic, then splash in the wine. Add the tomatoes and season. Bring to the boil. Reduce the heat, cover the pan and simmer for 5 more minutes, or until the beans are just tender. Garnish with the fresh coriander.

GOLDEN PILAFF WITH CORIANDER

Serve this elegant rice dish from Turkey with barbecued chicken or lamb kebabs. It will also complement other dishes very well, and any cold left-over rice can be turned into a delicious salad by adding some finely chopped vegetables and a vinaigrette dressing. The almonds can be toasted in a hot, dry frying pan. Vegetarians can replace the chicken stock with vegetable stock. This makes enough for 4 people.

350 g/12 oz/1³/₄ cups long-grain rice
450 ml/1 pint/2 cups chicken stock (broth)
generous pinch of saffron strands
salt
40 g/1¹/₂ oz flaked almonds, toasted
2 spring onions (scallions), washed and thinly sliced
handful of fresh coriander, washed and chopped

Soak the rice in plenty of fresh water, squeezing gently with your hand to release the starch. Rinse several times and drain well.

Bring the stock to a simmer in a pot with a lid. Add the saffron, season with a pinch of salt, turn off the heat and leave to infuse for 10 minutes. Add the drained rice and bring to the boil. Cover tightly, reduce the heat to minimum and cook very gently for 15 minutes. Gently mix in the toasted almonds, spring onions and coriander, and allow the rice to rest for a few minutes before serving.

SCRAMBLED EGGS WITH SAFFRON AND CORIANDER

Serve these delicious, golden scrambled eggs with warm Indian *nan* or *chapatis*. Alternatively, spoon the eggs into warm *pitta* bread pockets. They are best served straight away while still piping hot, but may also be eaten cold. This recipe makes an exotic breakfast, brunch or light lunch for 2 people.

pinch of saffron
3 tbs hot water
4–5 very fresh, free-range eggs
40 g/ 1½ oz butter
white parts of 2 spring onions (scallions), chopped
1 fresh chili pepper, seeded and chopped
salt and freshly milled black pepper
small handful of coriander leaves, washed and chopped

Steep the saffron in the hot water for 15 minutes. Lightly beat the eggs with the saffron liquid and set aside. Put half of the butter into a non-stick frying pan and gently fry the spring onions and chili for 1 minute. Pour in the egg mixture and scramble, initially over a medium heat, and then more gently. Scrape and stir constantly with a fork to obtain an even, fluffy consistency. Season, stir in the remaining butter and the coriander before the eggs have set completely, and serve while the eggs are still slightly moist.

TOMATO AND CORIANDER SALSA WITH TACOS

Serve this tangy, pungent raw *salsa* in warmed corn *taco* shells, which commercial brands are widely available. Only really ripe, fresh tomatoes should be used. Top with grated cheese, garnish with shredded lettuce and you have an instant Mexican snack. If you want a more substantial dish, first pile a layer of re-fried beans (see the recipe) into the *taco* shells, cover with *salsa* and finish with grated cheese and some lettuce. When fried eggs are also served, this more substantial dish is called *huevos rancheros*, which means 'rancher's eggs'. Both recipes make enough for 4 people.

SALSA
800 g/1³/₄ lb ripe tomatoes
1 tbs olive oil
white parts of 2 spring onions (scallions), thinly sliced
1 clove of garlic, peeled and finely chopped
a few drops of wine vinegar or lemon juice
4-6 hot green chili peppers, washed, seeded and thinly sliced
salt and freshly milled black pepper
generous handful of fresh coriander, washed and chopped

Immerse the tomatoes in boiling water for 30 seconds, refresh them in cold water and slip off the skins. Chop the flesh as finely as possible. Combine all the ingredients thoroughly in a bowl, cover and set aside for an hour or more to allow the flavours to develop.

RE-FRIED BEANS
1 onion, peeled
6 tbs vegetable oil
800 g / 1³/₄ lb canned red kidney beans
225 ml / 8 fl oz / 1 cup water
salt and freshly milled black pepper

Halve the onion from top to bottom. Slice each hemisphere thinly. Soften the sliced onion in half of the oil and set aside. Rinse and drain the kidney beans. Place them in a large, heavy frying pan, add the water and bring to the boil. Cook until almost all the liquid has evaporated, then remove from the heat and mash the beans to a coarse paste. Add the remaining oil and the fried onion, re-heat the pan and fry the beans, turning them constantly for about 5 minutes. Season and allow them to cool, or serve warm.

25

$\mathcal{S}$PICY FRIED NOODLES
WITH CORIANDER

Combining sweet, sour, hot and salty flavours (the fresh coriander contributing a warm tang,) these oriental noodles taste quite delicious. If fresh noodles are unavailable, dried ones can be substituted, but before they are added to the wok they must be reconstituted in boiling water as directed on the packet. Serves 4 people.

6 spring onions (scallions), washed
175 g/6 oz oyster or shiitake mushrooms
4 tbs peanut oil
4 cloves of garlic, peeled and chopped
6 fresh red chili peppers, washed, seeded and sliced
1 tbs tomato ketchup
2 eggs, beaten
5 tsp sugar
juice of ½ lemon or a lime
2 tbs Thai fish sauce or soy sauce
900 g/2 lb fresh egg noodles
or 350 g/12 oz dried noodles, reconstituted
175 g/6 oz bean sprouts
1 lemon or lime, quartered
110 g/4 oz peanuts, crushed
1 tsp cayenne
generous handful of fresh coriander, washed and chopped

Slice the spring onions thinly, separating the white and green sections. Slice the mushrooms.

Heat the oil in a wok and add the garlic. Stir once, then add the white spring onion sections and the mushrooms. Add the fresh chilies, tomato ketchup, eggs, 3 tsp of the sugar, lemon or lime juice, and fish or soy sauce. Stir-fry the mixture until the eggs begin to set. Add the noodles, half of the bean sprouts and toss constantly for 2 more minutes to heat through. Transfer to a warm serving dish.

Arrange the remaining bean sprouts around the edges, garnish with the lemon or lime quarters, and sprinkle the peanuts, cayenne, the remaining sugar, coriander and the green spring onions on top. Serve immediately.

STIR-FRIED VEGETABLES WITH CORIANDER

This colourful oriental recipe is healthy, nourishing and very easy to prepare. Accompanied by rice it makes a delicious complete meal for 4 people.

4 eggs
pinch of salt
3 tbs peanut oil
225 g/8 oz broccoli florets
225 g/8 oz baby corn
75 g/3 oz lean bacon,
trimmed and cut into thin strips
3 cloves of garlic,
peeled and finely chopped
4 shallots, peeled and chopped
225 g/8 oz small button mushrooms, left whole
salt
110 ml/4 fl oz/½ cup water
2 tbs light soy sauce
2 tbs Shaohsing wine or dry sherry
generous handful of fresh coriander, washed and chopped

Lightly beat the eggs with a pinch of salt. Heat 1 tbs of the oil in a wok and make an omelette with the eggs. Slice the omelette into finger-size strips.

Bring a pot of salted water to the boil. Blanch the broccoli and corn for 3–4 minutes. Remove and plunge them into cold water. Drain.

Heat the remaining oil in the wok. Add the bacon strips, stir-fry for 2 minutes, then add the garlic, shallots

and mushrooms; stir-fry for a further minute. Season, add the water, soy sauce, Shaohsing wine, strips of omelette and the blanched vegetables. Stir-fry for 3–4 minutes. Mix in the coriander and serve immediately.

SALMON STEAKS WITH TOMATO AND CORIANDER

These grilled (broiled) salmon steaks are accompanied by a delicious tomato and coriander sauce that is enlivened by a touch of chili and complemented by the warm, citrus flavour of fresh coriander. This is an easy dish for entertaining because the sauce can be prepared in advance and the salmon cooks very quickly. The quantities serve 4 people.

4 salmon steaks
olive oil
salt and freshly milled black pepper
900 g/2 lb ripe tomatoes
6 tbs extra virgin olive oil
1 onion, peeled and chopped
1 clove of garlic, peeled and finely chopped
1 dried red chili pepper, crumbled
pinch of sugar
glass of white wine
1 tbs lemon juice
handful of fresh coriander, washed and chopped
2 lemons, quartered

Coat the salmon steaks with olive oil and season them all over. Set them aside. Immerse the tomatoes in boiling water for 30 seconds, then refresh them in cold water, slip off their skins and chop finely.

Heat the extra virgin olive oil in a small pan. Soften the onion, then add the garlic, chili, chopped tomatoes, sugar, wine and lemon juice. Cover and simmer for 10 minutes.

30

Season. Strain through a wire sieve into a fresh pan. Over a high heat, reduce the volume of the liquid by half and set aside.

About 10 minutes before you are ready to eat, pre-heat the grill (broiler). When it is very hot, grill (broil) the salmon steaks for about 4 minutes on each side and transfer them to 4 warmed plates. Quickly re-heat the tomato sauce, stir in the coriander and spoon equal portions next to the salmon steaks. Serve immediately with a *pilaff* or boiled new potatoes and garnish with the lemon quarters.

'RED' CHICKEN CURRY

A vital ingredient in this deservedly popular and very fragrant Thai dish is home-made curry paste, intensely flavoured with spices and coriander roots. Oriental supermarkets sell ready-made Thai curry pastes but it is definitely worth making your own which will be fresher and more pungent. Make the full quantity as the surplus can be kept for a few weeks in a sealed jar stored in the refrigerator. Accompanied by rice and a vegetable, this dish serves 4 people.

RED CURRY PASTE
1 small red pepper, cap, pith and seeds removed
1 tbs small dried chili peppers or 10 large, milder ones
2 cm/1 inch piece of fresh ginger, peeled and chopped
1 stalk of lemon grass, chopped or grated rind of $\frac{1}{2}$ a lemon
4 cloves of garlic, peeled
6 coriander roots, washed (reserve the leaves)
6 shallots, peeled
1 tsp coriander seeds
1 tsp salt
1 tbs lime or lemon juice
1 tbs fish sauce
1 tbs peanut oil

Liquidize all the ingredients in a food processor (makes about 8 tbs).

CHICKEN CURRY

1 chicken
400 ml/14 fl oz/1³/₄ cups canned coconut milk
1 tsp salt
2 tsp sugar
2 tbs peanut oil
3 tbs red curry paste
1 tbs soy sauce
grated rind and juice of 1 lime or ¹/₂ a lemon
6 tbs water
175 g/6 oz fresh bean sprouts
reserved coriander leaves, chopped
2 sprigs each of basil and mint, washed
4–6 fresh chili peppers, seeded and thinly sliced

Remove the breast and leg meat of the chicken and cut it into small, even pieces. Combine in a pot with the coconut milk, salt and sugar. Bring to a simmer. Cover and simmer for 8–10 minutes, stirring occasionally.

Heat the oil to smoking point in a wok. Add the curry paste and stir-fry for 30 seconds to darken it. Stir in the soy sauce and citrus rind and juice, then add the chicken mixture, water and bean sprouts. Cook for 2–3 minutes, mix in the reserved coriander, the sprigs of basil and mint and serve immediately, garnished with the chilies.

33

FRIED CHICKEN WITH PEANUTS AND HERBS

All the ingredients for this recipe are available from oriental grocers or good supermarkets. The recipe serves 4 people, accompanied by rice and a stir-fried vegetable.

4 chicken breasts, skinned
small bunch of coriander, washed and chopped
1 stalk of lemon grass, chopped, or grated peel of $\frac{1}{2}$ a lemon
4 cloves of garlic, peeled and crushed
1 tbs fish sauce
1 tbs rice vinegar
1 tsp cayenne
1 tsp sugar
4 tbs peanut oil
50 g/2 oz peanuts
2 tbs soy sauce
4 fresh chili peppers, washed, seeded and sliced
2 sprigs each of basil and mint, washed

Cut the chicken breasts into 4 cm/$1\frac{1}{2}$ inch cubes and prick them all over with a fork or a sharp knife. Place in a bowl with half of the coriander and the remaining ingredients except for the oil, peanuts, soy sauce, chilies and herbs. Mix well, cover and set aside for at least 1 hour.

Heat the oil to smoking point in a wok. Stir-fry the marinated chicken for about 3 minutes, add the nuts and stir-fry for 3 more minutes. Add the soy sauce and stir-fry for another minute. Transfer the contents of the wok to a warmed serving dish. Garnish with the remaining coriander, the chilies, the sprigs of basil and mint, and serve.

FRIED CHICKEN WITH CORIANDER

This simple, homely Indian dish is delicious with rice, spicy vegetables and a little chutney. The quantities serve 4 people.

CORIANDER PASTE
3 cm/1¼ inch piece of fresh ginger, peeled and chopped
generous handful of fresh coriander, washed
4-6 fresh green chili peppers, washed and seeded
1 onion, peeled and roughly chopped
4 cloves of garlic, peeled
6 tbs water

Liquidize the ingredients and put the paste to one side.

CHICKEN
4 chicken breasts
freshly milled black pepper
4 tbs sunflower or peanut oil
salt
2 tbs lemon juice
110 ml/4 fl oz/½ cup strained yoghurt

Skin and quarter the chicken breasts. Season them all over with black pepper. Heat the oil to smoking point in a non-stick frying pan or wok. Fry the chicken until evenly golden, add the coriander paste and fry for 3 minutes. Season, add the lemon juice and yoghurt. Simmer, covered, for about 10 minutes, then serve immediately.

KHEEMA MATAR

This spicy, dryish dish of tender minced meat and vegetables is one of my favourite Indian recipes and owes much to Madhur Jaffrey. With her bestselling book and its accompanying television series, *Indian Cookery*, she taught many thousands of people how to cook, and above all appreciate, authentic Indian dishes. I have changed the original spicing and added some new potatoes to turn this into a hearty one-pot meal. Only very lean minced meat of the highest quality should be used, or a lot of fat will be shed. Serve with *nan* or *pitta* bread and an Indian pickle or chutney. The quantities are sufficient for 6 people.

DRY SPICES
2 tsp coriander seeds
2 tsp cumin seeds
6 cloves
2 tsp black peppercorns
2 tsp green cardamom pods
2 cm/1 inch piece of cinnamon

Toast the spices in a hot, dry pan until they darken slightly.
Transfer them to a clean coffee grinder or mortar and grind
them to an aromatic powder.

KHEEMA MATAR
3 tbs sunflower or peanut oil
1 medium onion, peeled and finely chopped
6 cloves of garlic, peeled and finely chopped
4 cm/1¹/₂ inch piece of fresh ginger, peeled and finely chopped
4 green chillies, seeded and sliced
2 tsp cayenne
225 g/8 oz small new potatoes, par-boiled
675 g/1¹/₂ lb lean minced beef
280 ml/10 fl oz/1¹/₄ cups water
350 g/12 oz frozen peas, thawed
2 handfuls of fresh coriander leaves, washed and chopped
salt
3 tbs lime or lemon juice

Heat the oil in a large, heavy frying pan. Add the onion and
sauté until lightly coloured. Add the garlic, ginger, chillies,
cayenne, potatoes, beef and half of the spice mixture. Stir-
fry over a medium heat for 5-6 minutes, to remove all trace
of rawness from the meat. Pour in the water, cover and simmer for 12–15 minutes, or until the meat is tender. Add the
peas and coriander, mix thoroughly and cook, uncovered,
for 5 more minutes. Season, add the lime or lemon juice,
the remaining spice mixture and cook for 1 minute longer.
Allow to cool and, if necessary, drain off any fat. Serve
warm or at room temperature.

BEEF IN CHILI SAUCE WITH CORIANDER

Fresh coriander complements this Chinese stir-fry admirably. All the ingredients are widely available in large supermarket branches or from Chinese grocers. Serve with plain boiled rice and an oriental vegetable dish. This is sufficient for 4 people.

MARINADE
675 g / 1¹/₂ lb (trimmed weight) rump steak
2 tbs Shaohsing wine or dry sherry
2 tbs light soy sauce
1 tbs peanut oil
3 tsp sesame oil
freshly milled black pepper

Removing all visible fat, cut the beef into strips, each about 5 cm/2¹/₄ inches long, 2 cm/³/₄ inch wide, ¹/₂ cm/¹/₄ inch thick. Mix the remaining ingredients in a bowl, add the beef, and set aside to marinate for an hour or longer.

CHILI SAUCE
2 tsp flour
110 ml / 4 fl oz / ¹/₂ cup water
3 tbs Chinese chili sauce
1 tbs rice vinegar
2 tbs soy sauce
3 tbs peanut oil
3 cloves of garlic, peeled and sliced
3 chili peppers, washed, seeded and thinly sliced
4 spring onions (scallions), trimmed and thickly sliced
generous handful of fresh coriander, washed and chopped

38

Mixing well, dissolve the flour in the water, chili sauce, rice vinegar and soy sauce. Lift the beef from the marinade with a slotted spoon. Heat the oil to smoking point in a wok. Add the garlic and chilies, mix once and add the beef. Stir-fry for 1 minute, add the spring onions and stir-fry for 1 minute longer. Pour in the chili sauce mixture. Toss for 3–4 more minutes or until the sauce has thickened. Transfer to a warm serving bowl, mix in the coriander and serve immediately.

ℬEEF CURRY WITH BAMBOO SHOOTS

Traditionally, this wonderful curry from northern Thailand
is prepared with wild boar, but rump steak makes an excellent substitute. Preserved bamboo shoots are sold in jars or
cans in oriental grocers. This recipe is for 4 people. Serve
with a stir-fried vegetable and rice or noodles.

CURRY PASTE
10 dried red chili peppers
4 red shallots (or 2 yellow ones), peeled
2 cloves of garlic, peeled
3 cm/1¼ inch piece of fresh ginger, peeled
2 stalks of lemon grass, chopped
grated peel of a lime
6 coriander roots, washed (reserve the leaves)
2 tbs peanut oil

In a food processor, grind all the ingredients to a paste. (This makes about 6 tbs – the surplus can be stored for a few days in the refrigerator.)

675 g/1¹/₂ lb rump steak
225 g/8 oz preserved bamboo shoots, rinsed and drained
6 tbs peanut oil
3 tbs curry paste (see above)
4–6 chili peppers, washed, seeded and thinly sliced
2 cloves of garlic, peeled and chopped
225 ml/8 fl oz/1 cup water
1 tbs fish sauce
1 tbs light soy sauce
2 tbs lime or lemon juice
2 tsp sugar
small handful of basil, washed
the reserved coriander leaves, washed and chopped

Removing all fat, cut the beef into chunks which should then be sliced thinly against the grain. Slice the bamboo shoots into strips.

Heat the oil to smoking point in a wok. Stir-fry the curry paste for 30 seconds (it will colour slightly). Add the beef, bamboo shoots, chilies and garlic and toss with the curry paste for 1 minute. Pour in the water, fish and soy sauces and the lime or lemon juice. Sprinkle with sugar and bring to the boil. Reduce to a simmer and cook gently for 10 minutes. Stir in the basil and chopped coriander and serve immediately.

CORIANDER